THE
LEGACY
of
PRAYER

Lois B. Johnson

authorHOUSE®

AuthorHouse™
1663 Liberty Drive
Bloomington, IN 47403
www.authorhouse.com
Phone: 833-262-8899

Published by AuthorHouse 01/17/2022

ISBN: 978-1-6655-2949-5 (sc)
ISBN: 978-1-6655-2948-8 (e)

Library of Congress Control Number: 2021924089

Print information available on the last page.

Any people depicted in stock imagery provided by Getty Images are models, and such images are being used for illustrative purposes only. Certain stock imagery © Getty Images.

Scripture quotations marked KJV are from the Holy Bible, King James Version (Authorized Version). First published in 1611. Quoted from the KJV Classic Reference Bible, Copyright © 1983 by The Zondervan Corporation.

This book is printed on acid-free paper.

Contents

Introduction!

Several years ago the Holy Spirit impressed upon my heart to write a book, specifically calling it with an unusual name! "The Legacy of Prayer"!!!! This book is and will always be special to me, as I attempt to explore the meanings of what "The Legacy of Prayer means to me. It is my very desire, that as you the reader, began this journey with me, you will develop an urgency and an unique life of prayer, that will hopefully become a part of your everyday life and continue for many generations to "follow!!! It is my desire that you will appreciate the communication that one has with God through developing a "A legacy of Prayer!!!! Many thanks go out towards great women and men of God that has been placed in my life, throughout the years, that allow God to use them and teach me the art of prayer! Mama Mary Ella, Mama Emma Jane, !!! (Children)Bee, Alvin, Donald, Roslyn, Melvin, Shirley, Christy, Sonia, Lois, Alan, Carol, Bishop, Ken, & Bishop, Gee, ! (We are the generation of children who are the products of those who prayed for us and left a legacy of prayer for us to follow) Note: We have passed on prayer to our seeds, our seeds to their seeds,. These are the "Mantel Catchers"

Note, Our-Children, Our- Grandchildren, Our-Great- grandchildren, and so on, and so forth, until the return of "Our Lord and Savior Jesus Christ"!!!! My prayer is that this legacy of prayer will always remain forever fervent in all hearts concern!!!!!

Chapter 1

WHAT IS PRAYER!

It is very important that in my discourse I give you the reader a clear definition of what "Prayer" consist of! Prayer can be labeled as the most sacred part of any believer's time wherein they commune with God!!! Prayer can be done or held in various ways! For example one can pray and develop a prayer life at home, at their place of worship, in a closed environment, or even while going about an every day daily routine ! Prayer is never limited to one or many circumstances. Prayer can be done individually, or collectively. The most vital part or point regarding prayer, is that "it is a sacred time with the creator of all "That being God himself!!

Chapter 2

WHERE AND HOW DOES HOW DOES PRAYER WORK!"

Prayer is usually done in a time of desperation, or when a tragedy take place. It can also be done during a time of uncertainty, or when one is worried about a certain or particular outcome! Many individuals pray, when they have been faced with an incurable disease, or an unusual death have taken place. Sometimes people are restless and cannot sleep, prayer have been used during such circumstances. Prayer has also been implemented as a time of introspection and transformation of one soul, spirit, and mind. Prayer has brought comfort and peace in many situations when there is no other means of conciliation or escape!!!!! Please remember that, the most vital part of prayer is, "your communication with God" as well the intimate time spent with the Lord!!!!!!! Prayer releases the spirit man from burdens that are overwhelming and difficult to bear!!!!! Prayer can be used anywhere, anytime, anyplace, and most of all with anyone, who is willing to invest their personal time of talking to the Savior!!!!! The Scripture tells of one mighty man of God, Daniel who prayed three times a day. (KJV) Daniel 6:10. This hero of prayer consulted God on a daily bases!!! He was attacked by his enemies due to his consistent prayer life!!!!! However, this did not discourage Daniel from praying to the Lord repeatedly!!!!!! Even to the point where he was thrown in the Lion's den for an undeniable life of prayer!!!!!

Chapter 3

HOW IS PRAYER EXECUTED!

Remember Jesus is the ultimate expert on prayer!! Even one of Jesus' disciples asked the question? "Lord teach us to Pray, as John also taught his Disciples! (KJV) Luke 11:1. Jesus had a quick response and gave a remedy of how to pray!

There were times in the Bible when Jesus himself prayed!. The Bible speaks of many times Jesus separating from his disciples and going to a sacred place of prayer! At his crucifixion, he utters words of forgiveness to his Father for those very ones who crucified him! This was done through prayer! Jesus instructs his disciples in the book of Luke 18:1 "that it is important that men ought always to pray and not to faint" (KJV)... Therefore if Jesus laid the pattern for prayer, it is essential that prayer is done on a consistent basis!!!! Simply, prayer must be practiced daily and routinely!!!! It must become a part of your everyday routine, that is followed and done without ceasing as commanded by our Lord! (KJV) Luke 18:1. Remember God Initiated Prayer. (Which started in eternity) Jesus is our Intercessor for prayer.(who Prayed for us in eternity) Holy Spirit carry out the command of prayer. (who executes the demands of prayer) ! God the Father, sanctions all and approves all demands of prayer! Prayer is executed through a daily routine and consistent reminder to touch bases with the creator!!!! We must always acknowledge the power of prayer!!!! Most recently l sat in a hospital office waiting for my Brother, who is the Bishop of our Ministry in New York City!!!!!! It was the department of "Radiation Oncology ! It was there l was personally able to whisper a prayer for my brother, and every patience that sat in that section, waiting for treatment!!!!!!! I was able to intercede for those who were believers, as well as those who were not!!!! My words of prayer were simple, for all those who passed by me "trust God, he is a healer"!Note! There were a multiple of individuals of all races present!!!!!!!! My prayer was at times silent, as l looked into the faces of those who were seated across from me, however, yet l believe effective!!!!! For l was executing my rights to pray!!!!! Silencing the Spirit of infirmities of "Cancers" of all degrees in the name of Jesus!!!!!!

Chapter 4

WHEN AND WHERE DID L LEARN TO PRAYER?

Please remember the name of my book "The Legacy of prayer"! As l stated before this book was written to inspire the reader on how to develop a love and urgency to pray. I first learn the art of prayer through two important woman in my life! One being my biological mother, secondly my stepmother. In which this book have been dedicated to both, who are now deceased. However, their legacy of prayer remains alive in me and my family today!!!! I can recall as a very young girl, seeing my biological mother, Mary Ella, kneeling down by a white cross, which hang over a bed in a two bedroom flat apartment in whom she raised 14 children! As a little girl l was very curious in finding out what was my mother doing kneeling every day at that wooden cross! Her routine was consistent, she never missed a day, l would peck around the half cracked door and listen to her says words of endearment to the Lord ! My biological mother, deceased at a very early age in life! Leaving behind 14 children ! However, her example of prayer never died with her, but remain very alive today in my life. My father remarried, when I was about 9 year old, to my stepmother, Emma Jane. It was as if God himself intervene and allow my siblings and l to go to another faithful women of God! Who would continue teaching us the principles of prayer! My stepmother, would call us in at a certain time of day! Specifically 6pm routinely, with an echo "Prayer Time"! These two words would ring out with such a unique sound that no matter where or how far my siblings and I were, we would come running from all directions to get home for prayer!!! This constant routine developed into a life time experience for me even to where l and my siblings prayer on a consistent basis daily!!

Chapter 5

HOW DOES PRAYER BECOME A LEGACY?

Prayer become a Legacy when it is rehearse from generation to generation! As any good inheritance, that are passed down ! Whether money, houses, businesses, cars, jewelry, what ever the costly and valuables are. If it has meaning and value, one will ensure its value. You will treasure its worth and cherish its memories! You will certainly make sure the next generation get a clear understanding of how much your inheritance is worth. You will even protect its cost legally through a jurdisal system as well as any means necessary. Prayer is more essential than any materialistic substance and last throughout ones life time and prepares one for Eternal life in the life to come. Prayer becomes a legacy when it is taught and passed down to the generations, that follows!!!! Note: if presented and practiced daily, to the recipient, then it can become a legacy that never dies! I can recall raising my two offsprings, Kim & Anthony, practicing similar models of prayer in which my mothers taught me!

Implementing a daily routine of prayer with role modeling what my mothers showed me! Today both my children have a fervent history of prayer! I recall visiting my daughter's home, lying in bed, Hearing her giving her two children, words of prayer of protection over their lives, prior of them leaving for school. My mind quickly went back to the times I taught her, and her brother, how to prayer each day, before leaving for school, and my mothers teaching me how to prayer, therefore, I now know, that this Legacy of Prayer will follow from generation to generation!!!

Chapter 6

WHAT ARE THE "7" P'S ASSOCIATED WITH PRAYER!

There are certain P's connected to the legacy of having a prayer life!

- 1. The Pleasure of Prayer!
- 2. The Presence of Prayer!
- 3. The Privacy of Prayer!
- 4. The Passing on of Prayer to the next Generation!
- 5. The Promises in Prayer!
- 6. The Power of Prayer!
- 7. The Protection of prayer!

The pleasure of prayer comes with an intimate life style of prayer with your Heavenly Father ! The presence of prayer is knowing that through prayer there is his Devine protection! That protection from God the father, never leaves his children, and is always near!!!! The privacy of prayer is knowing that God knows your thoughts and it will remain in confidence! The passing on of prayer is having the reassurance that your children and their children are in the mind of God ! The Bible tells us in the book of Deuteronomy chapter 7:9 (KJV) that God is faithful and he keeps his covenant and mercy with them that love him and keep his commandments to a thousand generations. What a promise of prayer? That if we be faithful to God, he then will be faithful to us even to a thousand generations; The power of prayer comes with using our God giving Authority. Prayer comes with power that will turn Mourning into Dancing! Sadness into Joy! Heaviness into Praises!! And the Putting forth a Hollowing that God himself will recognize !!!!! These "7" P's of prayer are all unique and should be implemented with our daily communication with God.

Chapter 7

"WHY SHOULD PRAYER CONTINUE AS A LEGACY"?

The Bible tells us in the book of Romans 12:12(KJV). Rejoicing in hope; patient in tribulation; "continuing instant in prayer"! The words that Apostle Paul states in his writing is an order of continuance ! Meaning one should always pray! Prayer must be implemented for every situation, regardless of the length, depth, width, or intimacy of the problem being prayed for. Pray if continued, would eventually become a Legacy!!! Please Note: The more one prays, the love and appreciation for prayer will become habit forming!!!! It will develop into an everyday routine, that becomes as personal to the individual Christian as does their every daily routines. Prayer will continue as a legacy, due to the Holy Spirit position, whom lives inside the believer and whose job is to bring all things to their memories and reminds them to pray always! The developmental of Legacy and continue prayer is conjunctive. It goes hand in hand!! I say this as I have two personal prayer partners Carol, and Shirley! (My Sisters)!! We have been instant in pray for years now! We have a routine and time of prayer that have develop over the years. It is a routine of praying three times a day. We pray specifically Morning, Noon, and Evening! That is at 9:0clock, <u>12:00 noon</u>, and Lastly, for the day <u>3:00 pm</u>. This simple routine, mind you, have been going on between me and my, co-prayer partners for decades, which We inherited this from our mothers. My children inheriting this practice from seeing me pray. During our time of prayer we have experience the presence of God's Devine favor, and his untimely protection over our lives. We have now witnessed our children praying daily with their children and using the same method and legacy with their children. Our constant prayer is that the God that we pray to daily, will continue to show himself merciful through prayer with the generations to follow as he promised in his word! (Deuteronomy 7:9 KJV).

Chapter 8

"WHAT BENEFITS ARE THERE IN KEEPING A LEGACY OF PRAYER"?

Like any good job, when applying one would inquire about the salary, benefits, the position it self and lastly, what will l take away from the job !!!!! Well there are "Benefits" associated with keeping the legacy of prayer!!!! And for those who are persistent in their personal relationship with the Savior, and have made him Lord of their lives!!!! They can be listed as you the individual will develop wages in heaven that does not match any salary given in the natural upon the earth!!! Yes, You will be paid for what you do for Christ in the supernatural realm!!!!! As in the natural realm, one will definitely inquire what retirement benefits can l achieve from my applied position!!!! Well in the spiritual realm, the retirement benefits for those the believer, who have invested in a sincere prayer life while on earth. Note:

Their Retirement Benefits comes with a package of the following!!!!

Eternal Life!

Everlasting Home with Christ throughout Eternality !

Ever being in the presence of God himself!

Escaping the wrath of eternal death!

Enjoying in with the heavenly hosts of angels in worshiping our Savior for a life time!

Ever dwelling with love ones and those whose names also have been placed in the Book of life! Knowing that your seed will carry on this legacy! A benefit of prayer is, to hear my daughter "Kim Monique" pray, and my son "Anthony Lance" pray, l know that this Legacy of prayer instilled in them from birth, still exist, after fifty odd years! What a benefit! These are just a few benefits that comes with developing a continuing life of prayer!!!

Chapter 9

"THE TIMES & TYPES OF PRAYERS THAT REMAIN ALWAYS"!

The times of prayer may vary! There are times when you the believer may be called to a solidarity place of prayer! When you are all alone in the very presence of God! Most recently l have been directed to go to my church at a certain time and lay on the altar alone!!! At this time l have experience such a peace that passes all understanding! l have at times been so overwhelmed with the cares of life which pushes me to a secret place for prayer! I can recall many nights of waking up and being led by Holy Spirit to pray!! Holy Spirit has led me to intercede, For many souls and individuals in my secret time of prayer! There have been souls who have been incarcerated that l have been directed to intercede on their behalf! Many individuals who have had cancers, diabetes, and other serious illnesses, Holy Spirit has led me to pray for and with! There is also in a legacy of prayer something called "the urgency of prayer"! This type of prayer comes with a press to prayer, and does not let up until until you are obedient and move to a secret place of prayer! With this type of prayer, It "wars off demonic attacks from the pits of hell"! There are certain warnings that Holy Spirit gives to the believer to intercede for a battle in the spirit realm!!! For the Bible says we "Wrestle Not Against Flesh and blood, but against Powers and Principalities and Wickedness in high places of darkness in this world"! Therefore, we must be equipped to do battle in the spiritual realm when and if necessary! You must continue in prayer, until "Victory" over the given situation is achieved!!!

Chapter 10

"JESUS CHRIST THE PERFECT ROLE MODEL OF LEAVING A LEGACY OF PRAYER!

In adapting an example of one who can be labeled as the perfect role model of Prayer! It would be Jesus Christ himself! The Bible tells us in the word of God, that on many occasions Jesus slipped away to his Father and prayed! One may ask the question, Why was it necessary for Jesus to Pray? Or even better what drove Jesus to Pray? I believe his incarnation, God in flesh, felt the need to be close to his Father, as he had never been separated from God before. He had special communicate with his beloved father, while being on earth. Remember Jesus' words "l do nothing on my own, but by the Father. Who sent me" Note: this dependency of his Father for all things drove him to seek God his Father for Devine instructions while on earth. Because of Jesus 'intense and periodic involvement of prayer throughout his life time. We know have a perfect role model, who not only prayed, but showed his followers the importance of having a long lasting prayer life with God his heavenly Father!!!!! While the world have many role models that are imitated daily. We the saints of God must depend on and rely wholly on the magnificent power of our perfect "Role Model ! Jesus Christ"!!!! Remember Jesus taught his Disciples to pray!!!!! (KJV) Luke11:1!!!!!! Therefore, We must continue his legacy!!

Conclusion!!!!!!!!

With the world in frequent crisis!!!! There is a need to continue praying!!!! I thought many years ago that thing we're going well with the world !!!! The economy was blooming, jobs were in command, money marketing was above the high level! Election were certain! Our children had models to follow! And most of all, the country was striving well! However, there have been such a reversal in all that were just mention!!!! We see more crime, more hatred world wide, more uncertainty about what the coming years would be like, with all types of diseases, mal- nutrition, homelessness, and most of all a lack or knowledge of the true and living God!!!!!! Yes it is necessary to continue to pray!!!! All who have offsprings, or younger generations to care for! It is vital to continue and practice praying!!! This legacy of pray must be universal, it must be worldwide, it must increase, it must never die, and most of all it must be sincere!!!!!!! For as the Bible Quotes!!! The fervent effectual Prayer of the righteous Avails Much! (KJV)!!!!!!!!!

I know there was a conclusion to this book!!!!!! However, most recently there was something that hit the country that is known as the conronvirus!!!!!

This is one of the most dangerous virus of all to hit the US!!! It has been so bad that, it Was necessary that l pull out my iPad and began to write another chapter to my book!!!! Please remember that my book was based on prayer!! A Legacy of Prayer!!!! I want to say prayer must be continued! Whether as "a family legacy", or as a nation legacy!!! "Prayer can not stop!!! It must be constant!!!! Meaning always, never ending, not ceasing, staying focus, staying in tune with the "Master" through the method and means of prayer. As faith is now, so must Prayer" be now!!!!! It can not stop!!!! It must be instant, it must be always !!!!! Just as the plague have invaded our territory, called the Coronavirus, we the people of God must invade the Lord with "Prayer" We cannot quit praying for an answer from God! In my generation l never imaging, that l would experience such a time as this in the year of 2020! My grandchildren in which are a total of 5, also have been witnesses of this virus and have join in with myself of sending up prayer every day. I never thought in my life time we as a family would have to be a part of a long legacy of instant prayer, asking God to heal a nation, in fact a whole world, who are momentarily in quarantine. As previously stated in my discourse, Prayer must be secured, and kept in a secret place always, as Psalm 91 says!!!!!! (KJV) "We never known when prayer has to be immediately put into practice!! Note ! what Psalm 91 says, He that dwelleth in the secret place of the most High shall abide under the shadow of the Almighty". Ironically the virus is called covid 19. I have reversed the number "19" and turned it into "91"! Specially the Psalm 91! Until there is a switch of good news and progress is made, we must continue to prayer, and abide under the shadow of the Almighty!!!!! Until there is a cure, declining in the hospital rates, declining in the number of deaths, in this present time(2020) from this virus, the church must continue to use the weapons we learnt, and was taught from our fore - parents as children, and that is the Legacy of Prayer!!!!! Remember, "Prayer is a Weapon"!!!!!!!

"The believer must have a "passion for prayer." l quote Elder Frank Gilmore in saying "we must pray to pray"! Just recently, listening to the "News" in New York City, which is where l reside and have been for the last 76 years. I heard our Governor say that the numbers of this dreadful virus has declined! In additions the numbers of both "hospitalization" and deaths from this virus is at its lowest since it was detected openly in NewYork City! I mention this in my book, due to the fact l have never experienced any thing more dreadful then this COVID 19 in my life time! Many of the people l knew personally were victims of this virus! Devoted Christians, from well known Bishops to every day members are no longer with us, but have gone on to be with the "Lord"! My point is that l had to rely on a group of prayer intercessors in which my Bïshop G. Seabrooks formulated. He instructed me to get a 24 hour prayer group of believers who would give of their time and prayed consistently for the virus as well as other essential needs during this time! I along with my sister Carol and brother in law Carl were in charged of the "Midnight" shift! I specifically chose this timing for l knew that we needed those who have a passion for prayer to take the charge over this hour! This being the most critical time of night! My mind would go back to the Bible when Paul and Silas prayed at midnight! (KJV)! "Miracles" happens when one prays at midnight! As a result of prayer, l am of the opinion that "God" hear the cries of the prayers going up before him.

Numbers of death and hospitalization in our areas began to decline! (note from the city, NYC) My point is that my sisters and l, come from a Legacy of Prayer individuals as mentioned earlier in my book! We were able to reminisce on prayers we heard our Mothers pray, and reflected on their legacy of praying! Oh yes, the Book of James 5:16 says "Confess your faults one to another, and prays one for another, that ye may be healed. The effectual fervent prayer of a righteous man availeth much" (KJV).

Progress of healing takes place in every aspect, when one learns to pray!

Printed in the United States
by Baker & Taylor Publisher Services